Best Chinese Take-out Recipes from Mama Li's Kitchen

Sarah Spencer

DISCLAIMER

All rights reserved. No part of this publication or the information in it may be quoted from or reproduced in any form by means such as printing, scanning, photocopying, or otherwise without prior written permission of the copyright holder.

Disclaimer and Terms of Use: Effort has been made to ensure that the information in this book is accurate and complete. However, the author and the publisher do not warrant the accuracy of the information, text, and graphics contained within the book due to the rapidly changing nature of science, research, known and unknown facts and internet. The Author and the publisher do not hold any responsibility for errors, omissions or contrary interpretation of the subject matter herein. This book is presented solely for motivational and informational purposes only.

CONTENTS

DISCLAIMER 3
CONTENTS 4
INTRODUCTION 8
APPETIZING TAKE-OUT SOUPS 11
   Sizzling Rice Soup 11
   Traditional Hot and Sour Soup 15
   No Fuss Egg Drop Soup 19
CLASSIC TAKE-OUT APPETIZER 21
   Traditional Pork Egg Rolls 21
   Vegetable Spring Rolls 25
   Dumplings with Peanut Sauce 29
   Spicy Peanut Sauce 33
   Shrimp Toasts 35
   Crispy Fried Wontons 39
   Shrimp Balls 41
   Kon Tiki Bobo Meatballs 43
   Tanguy BBQ Pork Short Ribs – Chinese style 45
VEGETARIAN TO GO 47
   Chinese Eggplant in Garlic Sauce 47
   Vegetable Egg Foo Young 51
   Mapo Tofu 55
   Buddha's Delight 57
   Hunan Bean Curd 61
   Green Jade Vegetables 63
RICE AND NOODLES 65
   Basic Fried Rice 65
   Yang Chow Fried Rice 67

 Chicken Chop Suey 69

 Chicken Lo Mein 71

 Beef Chow Mein 75

 Beef Chow Fun 79

CHINESE CHICKEN AND PORK MASTERPIECES ... 83

 Favorite Cashew Chicken 83

 Moo Goo Gai Pan 87

 Kung Pao Chicken 91

 Sweet and Sour Chicken 95

 General Tso's Chicken 99

 Pork with Snow Peas 103

 Mu Shu Pork 107

 Twice Cooked Pork 111

BEEF TAKE-OUT FAVORITES 115

 Beef and Broccoli 115

 Beef with Oyster sauce 119

 Pepper Steak 123

 Szechuan Beef 125

 Sesame Beef 129

 Kung Pao Beef 131

 Shrimp in Lobster Sauce 135

 Spicy Scallops in Garlic Sauce 139

 Cantonese Style Lobster 141

 Mu Shu Shrimp 145

MAMA LI'S SPECIALITIES 149

 Orange Beef 149

 Chicken Curry 153

 Lake Tung Ting Shrimp 155

 Chinese Spare Ribs 159

DESSERTS 161
  Almond Cookies 161
  Chinese Fortune Cookies 165
  Chinese Doughnuts 167
CONCLUSION 171
ABOUT THE AUTHOR 173
  More Books from Sarah Spencer 175
APPENDIX 177
  Cooking Conversion Charts 177

INTRODUCTION

Chinese food is possibly the most popular of take-out cuisines in America. Who can resist the glistening sauces hugging delicate little pieces of meat or crisp vegetables complimented by savory rice and noodles? Do you find yourself craving your favorite dish, but your favorite restaurant is too far away and you doubt that you would be able the master the many complex flavors in your own home well enough to be fully satisfied? The secrets of Chinese cuisine seem to be hidden in kitchens of small, family-owned restaurants where the owners will never tell their secrets. Well not up until now! In this book learn the secret recipes from Mama Li's kitchen.

Mama Li showed me everything I know about cooking Asian foods. One of the warmest memories I have from Mama Li was the patience she showed toward me when she hired me to assist in her restaurant's kitchen. She would carefully explain and show me how to choose the right ingredients at the market, handle the knife and chop quickly the fresh produces, prepare the secret sauce with just the right amount of spices and ingredients, stir-fry with the most amazing pan in my kitchen, the wok, how to use a bamboo steamer and so much more. I learned so much for those two wonderful years working for Mama Li. Since, then I have continued cooking like Mama Li showed me while adapting the recipes to my own family's preferences.

The beauty of Chinese cuisine lies in its simplicity. With a few ingredients rightfully chosen and flavorful spices, you can create the most amazing fresh meals in no time. You don't need to be an exceptional cook or have an immense pantry to enjoy your favorite takeout dishes fresh from your own kitchen. With a few simple ingredients, a couple of tools, and the desire to make your own Chinese takeout cuisine, you can soon be crafting these dishes for yourself.

Inside this book you will find Mama Li's authentic recipes for some of the most popular takeout choices, from fried rice to sesame beef, allowing you to indulge your craving easily, with little time or expense, not to mention the comfort of your own home and your own fresh ingredients. In addition, you will find recipes for some of the more elaborate Chef's creations so that you can prepare an elegant meal anytime for yourself, your family, or your guests. The recipes, the secrets, and a clear guiding hand are encased within the pages of this book. Read further to learn how to easily and masterfully create your favorite dishes, including soups, noodles, vegetarian dishes, chicken, pork, beef, and seafood. You get to handpick the ingredients and tailor them to your pallet. If you feel that your Chinese takeout meal just isn't complete without a fortune cookie, don't worry. We've included a recipe for those too.

Sarah

APPETIZING TAKE-OUT SOUPS

Sizzling Rice Soup

Serves: 4-6
Preparation Time: 15 minutes
Cook Time: 50 minutes

Ingredients

Soup Base

5 cups chicken Broth

1 cup chopped mushrooms, choose either shiitake or oyster mushrooms

1 teaspoon fresh grated ginger

¼ cup bamboo shoots

¼ water chestnuts

1 cup cooked shredded pork

1 tablespoon soy sauce

1 teaspoon rice vinegar

Crispy Sizzling Rice

½ teaspoon sesame oil (optional)

Crispy Sizzling Rice (make ahead of time)

1 cup long grain rice

1½ cup water or chicken stock

2 tablespoons peanut (or other preferred) oil

½ teaspoon salt (optional)

Directions

Crispy sizzling rice

- Due to the time involved, the crispy sizzling rice should be made ahead of time. Add rice to a medium-sized sauce pan. Add water or stock along with the salt, if desired. Bring rice to boil, and then reduce heat to a simmer, allowing rice to cook for 30 minutes. Preheat oven to 300°F/149°C while rice is cooking. If you choose a different style of rice for this dish, follow cooking instructions on the package.
- Once rice is cooked, spread it out on a baking sheet. It is OK if the rice sticks together. After the drying process, it can be broken off into pieces.

- Place the cookie sheet in the oven, and allow rice to oven dry for approximately one hour.
- Dried rice can be stored in an airtight container for several days.

Soup

- To prepare the soup, start by adding the chicken stock to a large soup pot. Cook while slowly increasing the heat to until broth begins to boil.
- Add shredded pork, ginger, water chestnuts and bamboo shoots to the broth.
- Reduce heat and let simmer for 5 – 10 minutes.
- After meat and vegetables have simmered for a few minutes, add in soy sauce, rice vinegar and sesame oil. Stir well to incorporate all flavors. Bring the temperature of the soup back up to a boil and then reduce heat to simmer. Let sit while the final preparations of the sizzling rice are made.
- Preheat a wok or small frying pan, and add the peanut oil for frying the rice. Once the oil is nice and hot, add the dried rice to the pan.
- Fry the rice, tossing gently, until it begins to puff and takes on a deep golden color.
- Remove rice from pan and allow oil to thoroughly drain off before adding to soup.

- For the best presentation, serve rice and soup separately at the table, either placing the rice in the soup for each guest or allowing them to add it themselves. As the rice is added a sizzling, crackling sound will be heard.

Traditional Hot and Sour Soup

Serves: 8

Preparation Time: 15 minutes

Cook Time: 30 minutes

Ingredients

8 cups chicken stock

1 cup chopped mushrooms, such as shiitake or oyster mushrooms

1-inch piece of fresh ginger, peeled and grated

¼ cup bamboo shoots, sliced

2 cloves garlic, smashed or diced

4 ounces cooked, shredded pork

1 package of firm tofu, diced

1 sheet dried seaweed

1 tablespoon garlic chili paste (adjust amount according to desired spiciness)

¼ cup soy sauce

⅓ cup rice wine vinegar

1 teaspoon sugar

2 tablespoons cornstarch, mixed with a little water to dissolve

1 large egg, beaten

1 tablespoon peanut (or other preferred) oil

Chopped green onions for garnish

Directions

- In a large wok or soup pot, add 1 tablespoon of peanut oil, garlic, ginger, pork, mushrooms, bamboo shoot, and garlic chili paste.
- Cook, stirring gently to incorporate all of the flavors, for 1 to 3 minutes.

- In a small bowl, combine soy sauce, rice vinegar and sugar, and toss into wok mixture.
- Cook for one minute longer to allow flavors to blend.
- Add chicken stock to the pan, increase heat, and bring soup to a boil
- Reduce heat and let simmer for 10-15 minutes.
- While soup is simmering, soak seaweed in some water until softened.
- Add cubed tofu and seaweed and cook for an additional 3-5 minutes.
- Add cornstarch mixture to the soup, stirring well to incorporate and to avoid the formation of clumps. Allow to simmer until soup begins to thicken.
- Once broth has thickened slightly, remove pan from the heat source.
- Stir soup in a constant circular direction, and slowly drizzle in beaten egg. This allows the egg to cook in thin, papery strips as opposed to thicker pieces. The egg will cook almost instantly once it is in the soup.
- Serve soup while hot and garnish with chopped green onions, if desired.

No Fuss Egg Drop Soup

Serves: 4

Preparation Time: 5 minutes

Cook Time: 15-20 minutes

Ingredients

6 cups chicken broth

2 tablespoons cornstarch

2 eggs, beaten

Chopped green onion to garnish (optional)

½ teaspoon salt

½ teaspoon pepper

Directions

- Add chicken broth to a soup pot, and heat to boiling.
- Season broth as desired with salt and pepper.
- While broth is boiling, mix cornstarch with enough cold water to thoroughly dissolve.
- Add cornstarch to broth, stirring to incorporate.
- Reduce heat, and let broth simmer for 5-10 minutes.
- Remove broth from heat source and let cool down slightly for approximately five minutes.
- Stir soup in a constant circular direction, creating a bit of a current in the liquid.
- Slowly drizzle the beaten eggs into the soup, allowing the eggs to cook in thin papery strips. Eggs will cook almost immediately on contact with the broth. To avoid clumping of cooked eggs, make sure there is movement in the broth and that the egg is not poured in too quickly.
- Serve immediately, garnished with green onion if desired

CLASSIC TAKE-OUT APPETIZER

Traditional Pork Egg Rolls

This is one of the most Classic Chinese egg rolls. It is a balanced mix of ground pork and vegetables. It is a tasty appetizer and a must-have for pork lovers.

Serves: 10 pieces
Preparation time:
Cooking time: 30 minutes

Ingredients

10 large egg roll wrappers

1 tablespoon cornstarch mixed in water to seal the egg rolls

Oil for frying

Pork filling ingredients

½ pound ground pork

Freshly ground black pepper

½ tablespoon soya sauce

½ teaspoon cornstarch

¼ teaspoon white sugar

Vegetable mix ingredients

2 garlic cloves, very finely minced

1 carrot, shredded, medium-sized

¼ head of green cabbage, shredded

5 shiitake mushrooms

1 teaspoon fresh ginger, grated

1 teaspoon Chinese rice wine

1 teaspoon soya sauce

2 tablespoons grape seed oil, separated

2 teaspoons rice wine

2-3 teaspoons soya sauce

¼ teaspoon sugar

Salt and black Pepper

1 teaspoon sesame oil

Directions

- Begin the preparation by marinating the filling. In a mixing bowl, combine all the ingredients for the ground pork, and let it marinate for 10 minutes.
- Grate the vegetables and the mushrooms.
- Coat a wok or a large frying pan with the grape seed oil on medium-high heat. Add the pork, and fry till the color changes. Remove the pork from the wok to a plate and set aside.
- Add grape seed oil and the vegetables to the wok. Begin with ginger and garlic, and follow with vegetables, stirring constantly.
- Once everything is fried and soft, add the sesame oil, rice wine, soya sauce, sugar, and black pepper. Cook for one minute on low heat.
- Finally, add the pork back in and mix everything. Cook for another minute.
- Remove from heat, and let it cool.
- Try and remove the extra moisture with paper towels.
- Spread the egg wraps on a flat surface. Fill each of them with one tablespoon of the filling.
- Roll and seal them perfectly using the water and corn starch mixture.

- Once done, cover the egg rolls with a clean, wet towel so that they do not dry.
- Refrigerate for 4 hours before frying them in oil. Serve with plum sauce or orange dipping sauce.

Vegetable Spring Rolls

Serves: 50

Preparation time: 45 minutes

Cooking time: 30 minutes

Ingredients

1½ cups bean sprouts

8 shiitake mushrooms

3 green onions, trimmed and diced

3 cloves, garlic, minced

1 teaspoon fresh grated ginger

2 medium carrot, shredded

2½ cups green cabbage, shredded

8 oz. canned bamboo shoots, drained and sliced thinly

2 tablespoons low-sodium soy sauce

1 tablespoon sesame oil

1 tablespoon cornstarch

2 tablespoons peanut (or any other preferred) oil

50 spring roll wrappers, thawed

1 egg, beaten with 2 tablespoons of water

Oil for frying

Directions

- Wash and drain the bean sprout. Set aside
- Wash and par dry the mushroom. Cut into julienne very finely.
- Heat 2 tablespoons sesame oil in skillet or a wok on medium-high heat. Add green onions, garlic, and ginger. Stir-fry for about 1 minute.
- Add remaining vegetables. Sauté until tender, about 3-4 minutes.
- Add soya sauce and sesame oil. Stir to combine well. Cook for 1 more minute and remove from heat.
- Place filling in a strainer to remove most of the cooking liquids. Place filling in a bowl.
- Open your package of spring rolls and place all but one wrapper under a clean, damp, dish cloth to ensure wrappers do not dry out.

- Set your wrapper on flat surface with one corner pointed at you.
- Place a generous tablespoon of filling on the bottom of the wrapper, about two inches above the corner point.
- Fold the bottom part of the wrapper over the filling, and then fold the sides over the filling, so you have what almost looks like an envelope with a long flap.
- Roll the spring roll away from you until you get about two inches from the top, brush the edges at the top with your egg wash, complete roll and repeat.
- Once you have all of your rolls set, line a plate with paper towels.
- Fill a heavy pot halfway up with oil for frying. Warm the oil on medium heat until it reaches 350ºF /177ºC. You can also use a wok or a deep frying machine. Deep fry spring rolls until golden, about 1-2 minutes on each side.
- Place spring rolls on a plate lined with paper towels to catch any excess oil before serving.
- Serve with your favorite dipping sauce.

Dumplings with Peanut Sauce

Serves: about 40 pieces
Preparation time: 1 hour 30 minutes
Cooking time: 30 minutes

Ingredients

1 pound ground pork

2 tablespoons soya sauce

1 teaspoon salt

1 tablespoon rice wine vinegar

¼ teaspoon white pepper

2 tablespoons sesame oil

2 tablespoons vegetable oil

3 green onions, sliced

1½ cups Napa cabbage, shredded

4 tablespoons bamboo shoots, shredded

1 teaspoon fresh ginger, grated

2 garlic cloves, minced

40-50 round dumpling wrappers

Egg wash for sealing (1 egg beaten with 1-2 tablespoons of water)

Directions

- Warm 2 tablespoons of vegetable oil in a wok on medium-high heat. Add the garlic and ginger. Sauté for 30 seconds. Reduce heat to medium and add the green onions, Napa cabbage, and bamboo shoots. Sauté until the vegetables are tender. Remove from heat and let cool down for a few minutes.
- Add the vegetable mixture to the raw ground pork. Mix well.
- Place 1 teaspoon to 1½ teaspoon of the pork filling onto one half of the wrapper. Seal the dumpling by brushing lightly with some egg wash on the edges. Press lightly to seal. Pleat if desired.
- You can cook the dumplings by either steaming (preferable for added flavors) or boiling them.

- When boiling, add them to the pot only when the water has started boiling. Let them boil for about 12 minutes.
- If you are using a bamboo steamer, place cabbage, bok choy or large lettuce leaves at the bottom of the steamer. It will prevent the dumplings from sticking to the bottom. Arrange the dumpling so they do not touch. Steam for 15 minutes.
- You can also fry them, after they have been boiled or steamed for added flavor.
- Serve with spicy peanut sauce (recipe follows). Serve warm.

Spicy Peanut Sauce

Yields about 1 ½ cup

Ingredients

½ cup smooth organic peanut butter,

1 cup water

1 tablespoon soy sauce

1 tablespoon hoisin sauce

1 teaspoon chili paste

1 pinch hot chili pepper flakes

Directions

- Combine ingredients in blender, mix until smooth.
- Add some more water if necessary for the desired consistency.

Note: this sauce can be very spicy depending on your chili paste. If you don't like spicy sauce, you can reduce the amount of chili paste and omit the chili pepper flakes. It is a good idea to taste the sauce and adjust the spiciness level to your own taste. You can start by adding only half of the chili paste and omit the chili pepper flakes. Then adjust to own liking.

Shrimp Toasts

Serves: 20

Preparation time: 15 minutes

Cooking time: 40 minutes

Ingredients

5 white sandwich bread slices

½ pound shrimp, shelled and deveined

1½ cups Napa cabbage, shredded

½ tomato, finely chopped

2 green onions, finely chopped

1 teaspoon fresh ginger, grated

1 tablespoon fresh coriander

1 tablespoon sesame oil

1 teaspoon rice wine vinegar or dry sherry

1 egg, beaten

Salt and pepper

2 teaspoons cornstarch

4 cups vegetable oil or more for frying

Directions

- Preheat the oven to 225°F/116°C and thaw the shrimp if they are frozen.
- Remove the crusts from the bread and cut each to for 4 triangles.
- Completely dry the bread by baking them for 10-15 minutes at 225°F/116°C, or until the bread is dry.
- Place the oil in a saucepan and warm on medium-high heat.
- In the meanwhile, place the remaining ingredients in the food processor. Pulse until you get a thick chunky paste.
- Take the bread out of the oven and let the toasts cool.
- Spoon the mixture evenly on top of each toast.
- In batches, add bread pieces into the hot oil. Place the toasts with a slotted spoon, shrimp mixture face down. Fry for about 1 minute, until golden brown. Turn the toasts over and fry for another minute, until golden brown.

- Remove the toasts and drain on paper towels.
- You can also bake these toasts, if you do not like to deep fry. To do so, heat the oven to 375°F/191°C and bake the toasts for 15 minutes, until golden brown.
- Serve while still hot.

Crispy Fried Wontons

Servings: 10

Preparation time: 10 minutes

Cooking time: 40 minutes

Ingredients

½ pound pork, ground

8 canned, water chestnuts, finely diced

¼ cup green onions, finely chopped

1 tablespoon soya sauce

1 teaspoon cornstarch

½ teaspoon salt

½ teaspoon ginger, grated

1 packet wonton skins

Oil, for frying

Directions

- In a mixing bowl, combine all the ingredients (except wonton skins and oil) to make a fine mixture. Mix well to ensure that all the ingredients are spread properly.
- Heat the oil on a medium heat in a saucepan. You can also use a deep fryer.
- Take a wonton skin, and lay it flat on a surface.
- At its center, place ¼ to ½ teaspoon of the mixture.
- Fold the wonton skin into half, covering the mixture.
- Seal the wontons by slightly pressing down to fasten the dough around the pork mixture, leaving the edges unsealed.
- Fry the wontons in small batches. Add the oil to a wok or large or a large frying pan and warm over medium-high heat. The oil should reach 350°F/177°C on an instant reading thermometer before cooking the wontons.
- Fry the wontons for around 2-3 minutes, until golden brown. Remove with slotted spoon and place on a plate lined with paper towels to drain excess oil.
- Serve hot or cold with a sweet and sour sauce.

Shrimp Balls

Serves: 35 balls

Preparation time: 40 minutes

Cooking time: 20 minutes

Ingredients

1 pound medium shrimp, shelled and deveined

8 water chestnuts, chopped

1 green onion, finely chopped

½ fresh ginger, grated

2 teaspoons soy sauce

1 teaspoon rice wine vinegar

½ teaspoon white sugar

¼ teaspoon sesame oil

Fresh grounded black pepper

1 egg white

½ teaspoon cornstarch

Directions

- Soak the shrimp in salted water for about 5 minutes.
- Rinse them with cold water and dry using paper towels.
- Mince both the shrimp and the chestnuts.
- In a bowl, mix all the ingredients to form a fine mixture.
- Make small balls of this mixture.
- Heat the oil in a frying pan on a high heat. Slowly add the shrimp balls to the pan and make sure not to crowd the pan.
- Fry the balls for 3-4 minutes or until they turn crisp and golden.
- Remove the balls from the oil and drain on a tissue paper.
- Serve the balls hot with a spicy sweet and sour sauce.

Kon Tiki Bobo Meatballs

Serves: 6-8

Preparation time: 30 minutes

Cooking time: 10 minutes

Ingredients

Meatball ingredients

1 pound ground pork

1 cup white bread crumbs

½ teaspoon ground ginger

¼ cup white sugar

1 garlic cloves, minced

Batter ingredients

1½ cup all-purpose flour

4 tablespoons white sugar

2 teaspoons baking soda

1 cup water

2 eggs

Salt and pepper

Oil for frying

Directions

- In a mixing bowl, combine all the meatball ingredients. Season with salt and pepper.
- Form meatballs of even sizes of about ¾ inch in diameter. Set aside
- To prepare the batter, mix the flour, sugar, baking soda. Season generously with salt and pepper. Pour the flour mix in a shallow dish.
- In another shallow dish, mix together the eggs, and water.
- Dip each meatball in the egg mixture and roll it in the flour mixture. Set aside on a plate.
- Heat the oil for frying or you can also use a deep frying machine. Fry the meatballs in batches for 5 minutes. Place on a plate lined with paper towel to drain the excess fat.
- Serve with cocktail toothpicks and a dipping sauce like sweet and sour or cherry sauce.

Tanguy BBQ Pork Short Ribs – Chinese style

Servings: 6-8
Preparation 30 minutes
Marinating time 8h00 or more
Cooking time: 1 hour

Ingredients
4 pounds pork spareribs

Marinade ingredients
3 tablespoons light Soy sauce
3 tablespoons dark soy sauce
⅓ cup hoisin sauce

1 tablespoon ketchup

1 tablespoon rice vinegar

2 teaspoons brown Sugar

½ teaspoon Chinese five-spices

2 garlic cloves, finely chopped

¼ cup honey

½ cup boiling water

Directions

- Prepare the ribs by removing the membrane with a pairing knife. Cut each rib individually. Set aside.
- Mix together soya sauce, hoisin sauce, vinegar, ketchup, chopped garlic, and brown sugar.
- Use this mixture to marinate the spare ribs and refrigerate it overnight.
- Next day, pre-heat the oven to 350°F/177°C.
- Mix honey with boiling water.
- Take a shallow roasting pan and add half an inch of water to it.
- Place this pan at the bottom of the oven.
- Now place the marinated rib directly on a rack above the water.
- Let the pork cook for 50 to 60 minutes.
- During the roasting process, brush the ribs with the honey water a few times.
- Remove from the oven and let it cool before serving.

VEGETARIAN TO GO

Chinese Eggplant in Garlic Sauce

Serves: 4

Preparation Time: 15 minutes

Cook Time: 15 minutes

Ingredients

5 Asian eggplants, cut into 1-inch wedges

½ cup vegetable broth

1 tablespoon sesame oil

2 green onions, sliced with white and green parts separated

1-inch piece fresh ginger, peeled and grated

3 garlic cloves, minced and crushed

1 fresh red chili, sliced

3 tablespoons soy sauce

2 tablespoons rice vinegar

1½ tablespoons brown sugar

1 tablespoon cornstarch

Toasted sesame seeds for garnish (optional)

Thai holy basil for garnish (optional)

1 tablespoon peanut oil

Rice for serving

Directions

- Heat a wok over high heat. Add peanut oil and coat pan evenly.
- To the hot wok, add a single layer of eggplant. Cook, tossing gently for 2-3 minutes. Depending on the size of your wok, the eggplant may need to be prepared in batches.
- Once eggplant is cooked through, remove from wok, and reserve.

- Add a small amount of peanut oil back into the wok. Add ginger, garlic, chili and white parts of green onions. Cook, tossing gently until ingredients start to let off a strong aroma, approximately 2 minutes.
- In a small bowl add soy sauce, brown sugar, sesame oil, vinegar and cornstarch together. Whisk until well mixed and free of any clumps from the cornstarch.
- Add broth and soy sauce mixture to the pan, cooking until the sauce has thickened slightly, approximately two minutes.
- Add eggplant back into the pan and toss to coat.
- Serve immediately with rice and garnish with sesame seeds and basil if desired.

Vegetable Egg Foo Young

Serves 4-6

Preparation Time: 15 minutes

Cook Time: 35 minutes

Ingredients

2 cups fresh shelled peas

2 cups mung bean sprouts, chopped

1 bunch green onions, sliced with green and white parts separated

2 medium carrots, shredded

10 eggs, beaten

1 cup vegetable broth

2 tablespoons mirin (see Tip, below)

3 tablespoons soy sauce

1 tablespoon cornstarch

½ teaspoon salt

½ teaspoon white pepper (optional)

1 tablespoon water

Cooking spray to coat

Directions

- Preheat oven to 350°F/177°F.
- Coat a round 9-inch baking dish with cooking spray.
- Whisk eggs and salt in a large bowl.
- Add peas, carrots, bean sprouts, and green onions.
- Spread mixture evenly in the baking dish.
- Place in oven and bake for approximately 30 minutes or until edges are starting to brown.

- While the omelet is cooking, prepare the gravy: In a medium saucepan add broth, mirin, soy sauce and white pepper (optional) and bring to a boil. Reduce heat to medium-low and simmer for 5 minutes.
- Combine cornstarch and water in a small bowl and whisk until smooth. Add cornstarch mixture to hot broth. Continue cooking over low heat for several minutes, stirring occasionally until sauce thickens.
- When cooked, remove the egg foo young from the baking dish and plate.
- To serve, either pour gravy over the egg foo young, or serve on the side.

Mapo Tofu

Serves: 4

Preparation Time: 15 minutes

Cook Time: 15 minutes

Ingredients

14 ounce block of silken tofu, drained and cut into ¾" cubes

½ cup chicken broth

2 cups broccoli florets

2 teaspoons soy sauce

1 tablespoon sesame oil

1 teaspoon sugar

2 medium cloves of garlic, crushed and minced

1-inch piece of ginger, peeled and grated

4 green onions white part only, minced

1 tablespoon black bean paste

2 teaspoons chili bean paste

1 teaspoon cornstarch

Green part of green onions minced for garnish

Rice for serving

Directions

- In a small bowl, mix chicken broth, soy sauce, sugar, and cornstarch. Whisk until well blended and free of any clumps
- Heat a wok over high heat. Add sesame oil, garlic, ginger, broccoli, and green onions. Cook, tossing gently, until broccoli begins to turn a brighter green and aroma becomes fragrant. Stir in black bean paste and chili bean paste. Toss gently.
- Add cubed tofu to the wok. Toss gently before adding the entire broth mixture. Continue cooking, bringing sauce to a boil. Reduce heat, and cook for two minutes, or until sauce thickens
- Garnish with green onions, if desired
- Serve with rice.

Buddha's Delight

Serves: 4-6

Preparation Time: 15 minutes

Cook Time: 20 minutes

Ingredients

5 cups broccoli florets

3 medium carrots, sliced thinly in a diagonal direction

1½ cups snow peas, washed and trimmed

1½ cups baby corn

1 cup water chestnuts

½ cup bamboo shoots

½ cup black Chinese mushrooms (shiitake), quartered

1 block extra firm tofu, cubed

1 bunch green onions, sliced, white and green parts separated

3 cloves of garlic, crushed and minced

2-inch piece of fresh ginger, peeled and grated

2 tablespoons soy sauce

2 tablespoons rice vinegar

½ cup vegetable broth

1 tablespoon cornstarch

1 teaspoon sugar

½ teaspoon salt

2 tablespoons peanut (or other preferred) oil

Rice to serve

Directions

- Blanch broccoli and carrots in boiling water for 2 minutes, remove and submerge into cold water to stop cooking.
- Heat a wok over high heat. Add peanut oil and tofu. Cook, tossing gently until tofu just begins to brown around the edges.
- Add in garlic, ginger, salt, and green onion (white parts only). Toss with tofu, cooking for one minute.
- Add broccoli, carrots, snow peas, water chestnuts, baby corn, mushrooms, and bamboo shoots. Toss with fragrant tofu mixture over high heat for 2 minutes.

- In a small bowl, combine vegetable stock, soy sauce, rice vinegar, sugar and cornstarch. Mix well with a whisk until free of any clumps.
- Add liquid to pan and bring to boil for one minute. Reduce heat to a simmer and continue to cook for 3-5 minutes or until sauce begins to thicken.
- Serve immediately with rice, and garnish with green onions if desired.

Hunan Bean Curd

Serves: 4

Preparation Time: 15 minutes

Cook Time: 20 minutes

Ingredients

1½ 14-ounce blocks extra firm tofu, cubed

2 cups broccoli florets

1 cup shiitake or any Asian mushrooms, cut into large pieces

3 cloves garlic, crushed and minced

½ teaspoon soy sauce

2 teaspoons sherry

1 teaspoon sesame oil

1 cup vegetable stock

1 teaspoon chili bean paste

2 teaspoons crushed red pepper

½ teaspoon cornstarch, mixed with enough water to form a thin paste

½ teaspoon salt

1 tablespoon peanut (or other preferred) oil

Rice for serving

Directions

- Heat wok over high heat, and add enough oil to lightly coat pan.
- Toss tofu into hot pan, stirring continuously until tofu begins to brown. Remove tofu from pan and set aside.
- Add broccoli, bean paste and crushed red pepper to the wok. Cook while tossing gently for about 2 minutes.
- Add mushrooms and garlic, cooking for one minute before adding vegetable stock.
- Return tofu to pan. Add soy sauce, sherry and sesame oil. Cook for 1 minute.
- Add cornstarch mixture to the pan and cook for 3 minutes or until sauce begins to thicken. Season sauce with salt if desired. Serve immediately with rice, and garnish with green onions if desired.

Green Jade Vegetables

Serves: 4-6

Preparation Time: 15 minutes

Cook Time: 15 minutes

Ingredients

3 cups broccoli, chopped, including stems

2 cups snow peas, rinsed and trimmed

2 cups mini bok choy, rinsed and trimmed

2 cloves of garlic, crushed and minced

1 onion, diced

1-inch piece of fresh ginger, peeled and grated

3 tablespoons rice wine vinegar

4 tablespoons low-sodium soy sauce

½ tablespoon sesame oil

½ cup water

1 teaspoon sugar

1 tablespoon cornstarch

½ teaspoon salt

2 tablespoons peanut (or other preferred) oil

Rice for serving

Directions

- In a large saucepan, filled with boiling water, blanch bok choy and broccoli for 2 minutes. Drain under cold water to stop the cooking process. Set aside.
- In a small bowl combine sugar, water, soy sauce, sesame oil, and cornstarch. Set aside.
- Heat wok and add 1 or 2 tablespoons of peanut oil over medium-high heat. Add onions, garlic and ginger. Cook for one minute.
- Add broccoli, snow peas, and bok choy. Cook for 3-4 minutes, tossing gently, until vegetables begin to soften just slightly and become brighter in color.
- Add rice wine vinegar and cover to let the vegetable steam the wine fragrance. Cook for 1 minute.
- Add soy sauce mixture to pan and cook only until sauce begins to thicken. Season with salt if desired. Serve immediately with rice.

RICE AND NOODLES

Basic Fried Rice

Serves: 4-6

Preparation Time: 10 minutes

Cook Time: 15 minutes

Ingredients

3 eggs, beaten

3 cloves garlic, crushed and minced

2-inch piece of ginger, peeled and grated

1 bunch green onions, chopped, greens and whites separated

¼ pound cooked crumbled bacon or pork

3 tablespoons soy sauce

½ teaspoon salt

½ teaspoon pepper

8 cups cooked long grain rice

2 tablespoons peanut (or other preferred) oil

Directions

- Warm the wok on medium-high heat. Add 1 tablespoon oil to the hot wok, and quickly scramble eggs, cutting into small pieces while cooking. Remove eggs from pan and set aside.
- Add the remaining oil to the pan and then add garlic, ginger, green onions, and pork. Toss gently until fragrant, approximately 1 minute. Season with the salt and the pepper.
- Add rice to pan, tossing with garlic mixture to evenly incorporate and toast rice.
- Add soy sauce and eggs to rice mixture, toss gently while cooking for 1 minute.
- Serve immediately.

Note: for best results, cook rice a day ahead of time or use left over rice.

Yang Chow Fried Rice

Serves: 4-6

Preparation Time: 20 minutes

Cook Time: 15-20 minutes

Ingredients

2 eggs, beaten

⅔ cup frozen peas, thawed

1 medium carrot, diced

½ pound Chinese roast pork, cooked, shredded, or diced

½ cup small shrimp, shelled and deveined

3 cloves garlic, crushed and minced

3 green onions, sliced, whites and greens separated

4 tablespoons soy sauce or ponzu

4-5 cups cooked rice

1½ tablespoons peanut (or other preferred) oil

Directions

- Heat 1 tablespoon of oil in a wok over medium-high heat.
- Add eggs and cook until just set, cutting into small pieces while cooking. Remove from pan and set aside.
- Add garlic and vegetables to pan, and cook for 4 minutes, tossing gently while cooking.
- Add remaining oil and shrimp to the pan, and cook until they begin to turn pink and look done. Add pork, remaining oil, and egg back into to the pan, tossing gently to incorporate. Cook for about 2 minutes.
- Add rice and soy sauce to pan. Cook rice, tossing gently until well incorporated and rice begins to toast very slightly, approximately 3-4 minutes.
- Serve immediately, garnishing with green onions if desired.

Note: for best results, cook rice a day ahead of time or use leftover rice.

Chicken Chop Suey

Serves: 4

Preparation Time: 10 minutes

Cook Time: 15 minutes

Ingredients

1 pound boneless, skinless chicken, cubed

2 cups bean sprouts

½ cup shiitake mushrooms, chopped

½ cup chopped celery, chopped

½ red bell pepper, julienne

½ green bell pepper, julienne

1 yellow onion, diced

1 cup chicken stock

2 tablespoons low sodium soy sauce

2 tablespoons cornstarch

¼ cup water or more if needed

2 tablespoons peanut oil

Directions

- Heat oil in a wok over medium-high heat. Add chicken and onions, cooking while stirring for 5-6 minutes.
- Add celery, green and red bell peppers, mushrooms, bean sprouts and chicken stock to the pan. Bring to a boil, then reduce heat to medium-low and simmer 5 minutes.
- Mix cornstarch and water together, whisking until smooth and free of any clumps. Add cornstarch mixture to pan and cook an additional 5 minutes, or until sauce thickens.
- Remove from heat and serve immediately.
- Serve immediately

Chicken Lo Mein

Serves: 4-6

Preparation Time: 10 minutes

Cook Time: 15 minutes

Ingredients

- 1 pound Chinese egg noodles
- 2 cups Napa cabbage, shredded
- 1 cup oyster mushrooms, chopped
- 5 green onions, sliced, greens part reserved for garnish

1 pound boneless, skinless chicken, cubed

1 tablespoon sesame oil

1-inch piece of ginger, peeled and grated

2 tablespoons soy sauce

2 tablespoons sherry

1 teaspoon cornstarch

½ teaspoon crushed red pepper

½ teaspoon salt

1 tablespoon peanut (or other preferred) oil

Directions

- Begin by cooking noodles: In a large sauce pan or stock pot, bring water to a boil. Add noodles and cook until firm, approximately 5 minutes. Check for doneness along the way, as cooking times may vary depending on thickness. Drain and rinse with cold water. Return noodles to pot, and toss gently with sesame oil. Set aside.
- Heat a wok over high heat and add oil to coat pan.
- Add crushed red pepper to the pan, tossing around until fragrant. Add chicken, ginger, soy sauce, sherry, salt, and cornstarch. Cook, tossing gently, for 2 minutes.

- Add shiitake mushrooms, white parts of the green onions and cabbage, cook for two more minutes until chicken begins to brown and cabbage wilts slightly. Remove chicken mixture from pan and set aside.
- Add a bit more oil to the hot pan before adding noodles. Toss noodles in the hot oil for no more than 1 minute. Add the chicken mixture back into the pan and toss gently until heated through.
- Garnish with green onions, if desired.
- Serve immediately

Beef Chow Mein

Serves: 4-6

Preparations: 35 minutes

Cook Time: 15 minutes

Ingredients

1 pound flat iron steak, sliced

1 egg beaten

½ cup oyster mushrooms

½ cup bamboo shoots, sliced thinly

1 medium carrot, sliced on the diagonal

1 cup bean sprouts

5 green onions, sliced, with greens part reserved for garnish

2 tablespoons soy sauce

1 tablespoon sugar

2 cups beef stock

2 tablespoons cornstarch

1 teaspoon sesame oil

2 cups dry Chinese egg noodles

1 tablespoon peanut (or other desired) oil

Directions

- Begin by preparing meat and marinade: In a medium-sized bowl, mix soy sauce and sugar until well dissolved. Add meat and toss to coat. Cover and refrigerate for at least 30-60 minutes.
- In a small bowl, combine cornstarch and beef stock, whisking until free of clumps.
- Add sesame oil to a hot wok. Add steak to the wok and cook for 5 minutes (do not discard marinade).
- Add reserved marinade to saucepan along with the broth and cornstarch mixture. Bring liquid to a boil.
- Add all vegetables to the pan, tossing gently while cooking for 5 minutes. Turn down heat to a low simmer while noodles are being prepared.
- In a large sauce pan or stock pot, heat water to boiling. Add noodles and cook according to package instructions until firm but tender.

- Drain and rinse with cold water to stop the cooking process.
- Add noodles to wok, toss gently, remove from heat and set aside.
- In a separate pan, add peanut oil and cook beaten egg over medium heat. Let egg sit in pan while cooking to form a thin, omelet like covering. Cut egg into very thin strips.
- Place noodles on a plate, topped with sliced egg.
- Serve immediately.

Beef Chow Fun

Serves: 4-6

Preparation Time: 35 minutes

Marinating Time: 30-60 minutes

Cook Time: 20 minutes

Ingredients

Meat and marinade

1 pound flat iron steak, sliced thin

2 tablespoons soy sauce

1 egg white

2 teaspoons sesame oil

Sauce

2 tablespoons soy sauce

1½ tablespoons oyster sauce

2 tablespoons sherry

¼ teaspoon sugar

Other ingredients

½ pound Chinese egg noodles

½ green bell pepper, julienne

½ medium yellow onion, thinly sliced

1 cup bean sprouts

3 cloves garlic, crushed and minced

½-inch piece of ginger, peeled and sliced thinly

1 tablespoon black bean paste

1 tablespoon sherry

1 ½ tablespoon peanut oil

Directions

- In a medium bowl, combine marinade ingredients. Add meat, tossing to coat. Cover and refrigerate for 30-60 minutes.
- In a separate bowl, whisk together sauce ingredients until well blended and set aside.
- Heat wok over high heat. Add ½ tablespoon peanut oil to coat the pan. Add noodles, and toss gently while toasting until they just begin to brown. Remove from pan and set aside.

- Add ½ tablespoon peanut oil to the wok, and bring heat back up. Add garlic and ginger, cooking for 1 minute. Add sherry and black bean paste to the wok, stirring to incorporate.
- Add onion and pepper to the pan and cook for 2 minutes. Transfer onion and pepper mixture to another plate and set aside.
- Add remaining peanut oil to the wok, and add marinated meat. Cook, tossing gently until meat begins to brown. Add noodles and vegetables to the wok, and continue cooking while tossing. Add sauce mixture to the pan, coating ingredients thoroughly. Add bean sprouts right before serving.
- Serve immediately

Note: A good tip to slice the flank steak is to freeze it about 10-15 minutes before slicing. It will be much easier to make thin, even slices.

CHINESE CHICKEN AND PORK MASTERPIECES

Favorite Cashew Chicken

Serves: 4

Preparation Time: 15 minutes

Cook Time: 15 minutes

Ingredients

1½ pounds boneless, skinless chicken, cubed

½ small red bell pepper, cubed

1 cup raw unsalted cashews, chopped coarsely

5 garlic cloves, crushed and minced

5 scallions, diced, green parts reserved for garnish

2 tablespoons rice vinegar

3 tablespoons hoisin sauce

1 teaspoon honey

1½ tablespoons soy sauce

¼ teaspoon sesame oil

3 tablespoons water

1 tablespoon peanut (or other preferred oil)

½ teaspoon salt (optional)

½ teaspoon pepper (optional)

Small pinch cayenne pepper, if desired

Cooked rice for serving

Directions

- Preheat oven to 350°F/177°C.
- Spread cashews out onto a baking sheet, and toast in the oven for 5-7 minutes.
- Allow to cool completely before use.
- In a wok or large sauté pan, heat 1 tablespoon peanut oil to very hot. Add chicken, garlic, red bell pepper, white scallions, salt, pepper, and cayenne.
- Cook, tossing gently, until chicken is browned to a nice golden color, for 3-5 minutes. Do not cook the chicken thoroughly at this point, as that would result in an overcooked final dish.

- Depending on the size of the pan, you may have to cook the chicken in two batches in order to achieve an equal golden color on all pieces.
- In a bowl, whisk together the vinegar, hoisin sauce, soy sauce, honey, and sesame oil until well combined.
- Add sauce mixture to pan, and continue cooking until flavors are blended and chicken is cooked to the point where it is no longer pink and juices run clear.
- Remove from heat and toss in roasted cashews. Season with salt and pepper, if desired.
- Serve immediately with cooked rice, and garnish with scallion greens if desired.

Moo Goo Gai Pan

Serves: 4

Preparation Time: 15 minutes

Cook Time: 25 minutes

Ingredients

1 pound boneless, skinless chicken, cubed

3 cloves garlic, sliced

1-inch piece of fresh ginger, peeled and sliced thinly

1 cup mushrooms, chopped coarsely

¾ cup cabbage, sliced into thin strips

1 medium carrot, thinly sliced in a diagonal direction

1 generous cup snow peas, washed and trimmed

½ cup sliced green onion, whites and greens separated

½ cup water chestnuts

1 cup bamboo shoots

1½ cups chicken stock

2 tablespoons cornstarch

1 tablespoon peanut (or other desired) oil

Rice for serving

Directions

- Add peanut oil to preheated wok, or a large sauté pan.
- Add ginger and garlic to the pan and sauté until browned. This step is to add fragrance to the oil. Strain the ginger and garlic with a slotted spoon from the hot oil and discard.
- Add chicken and sauté over medium heat for approximately 5 minutes.
- While chicken is cooking, combine corn starch and chicken stock. Whisk until mixture is free of any clumps.
- Add cabbage, carrots, mushrooms, and snow peas to the pan. Sauté together for 3-4 minutes.
- Pour chicken stock mixture into pan. Bring contents to a boil, and then reduce heat to a low simmer.
- Add water chestnuts, bamboo shoots, and white parts of the green onion to the pan.

- Cover and simmer for 15-20 minutes until vegetables are a crisp tender.
- Remove from heat and serve with rice. Garnish with green onions if desired.

Kung Pao Chicken

Serves: 4

Preparation Time: 40 minutes

Cook Time: 20 minutes

Ingredients

Chicken and marinade

1 pound boneless, skinless chicken, cut into thin slices.

2 tablespoons soy sauce

2 tablespoons rice vinegar

1 tablespoon peanut oil

½ teaspoon sesame oil

½ teaspoon red pepper flakes

Cooking sauce

1-inch piece of fresh ginger, grated

3 fresh red chili peppers, seeded and halved

2 green onions, sliced, white parts only

2 cloves garlic, crushed and minced

½ cup roasted, unsalted peanuts

2½ tablespoons soy sauce

3 tablespoons rice vinegar

1 tablespoon plum sauce

1 tablespoon sugar or honey

1 teaspoon cardamom

¼ cup chicken stock

2 tablespoons corn starch

1 tablespoon peanut (or other preferred) oil

Rice for serving

Directions

- In a medium-sized bowl, combine all ingredients for the marinade. Whisk until thoroughly blended. Add chicken and stir until all pieces are coated. Cover bowl with a lid or plastic wrap, and refrigerate for 30-60 minutes.
- Heat a wok or large sauté pan over medium-high heat. Add peanut oil to hot pan.
- Into the hot oil, add the chilies, ginger, garlic, green onion.
- Cook while gently tossing for 1 minute.

- Add marinated chicken to the pan, including a little of the marinade if desired. Toss with other ingredients and cook for two minutes, then reduce heat to medium-low.
- Meanwhile combine soy sauce, plum sauce, vinegar, sugar, and cardamom in a small bowl. Whisk until ingredients are well blended.
- In a cup, combine chicken stock and cornstarch. Whisk until blended and free of clumps.
- Add chicken stock mixture to sauce. Blend and whisk.
- Add entire mixture to the pan, and increase heat to bring to a boil.
- Reduce heat, add peanuts, and allow contents to simmer until sauce thickens slightly.
- Serve immediately with rice if desired.

Sweet and Sour Chicken

Serves: 4

Preparation Time: 15 minutes

Cook Time: 25 minutes

Ingredients

1 pound boneless, skinless chicken, cubed

1 red bell pepper, seeded and cubed

1 green bell pepper, seeded and cubed

1 cup fresh pineapple, chunked

½ cup fresh pineapple juice

½ cup rice wine vinegar

¾ cup sugar

½ cup cornstarch, divided

2¼ cup flour

1 egg, beaten

1½ cups vegetable oil for frying

3¼ cups water

Rice for serving

Directions

- Begin by preparing sauce: In a medium sauce pan combine 1½ cups water, sugar, vinegar, and fresh pineapple juice.
- In a separate small bowl, combine half of the cornstarch and ¼ cup water. Whisk until blended and mixture is free of any clumps.
- Heat sauce in pan to boiling, and then remove from heat. Slowly add in cornstarch mixture, stirring until well incorporated and mixture begins to thicken slightly. Set Sauce aside.
- To make the batter: In a separate bowl, combine flour, 2 tablespoons of cornstarch, 2 tablespoons of oil, egg and salt and pepper as desired to taste. Whisk together until blended.
- Gradually stir in up to 1½ cups water until a thick batter is formed. Batter should be thick enough to cling to the chicken in a medium to thick coat.
- Add cubed chicken and toss until well coated.

- Heat frying oil over medium high heat in a wok or large sauté pan. It should reach 350°F/177°C on an instant reading thermometer.
- Once oil is hot, add chicken and cook for 10-15 minutes until chicken is crispy and golden brown.
- Remove chicken from pan and let excess oil drain off. Remove any leftover oil from the pan.
- Return chicken to the pan and add sauce, bell peppers, and pineapple chunks. Toss gently while heating over low heat.
- Serve immediately with rice.

General Tso's Chicken

Serves: 4

Preparation Time: 40 minutes

Cook Time: 20 minutes

Ingredients

Chicken and marinade

1 pound boneless, skinless chicken, cubed

2 tablespoons soy sauce

3 tablespoons sherry wine

2 tablespoons rice vinegar

2 tablespoons cornstarch

Sauce

¼ cup chicken stock

¼ cup soy sauce

2 tablespoons sherry wine

2 tablespoons rice wine vinegar

1½ teaspoons sesame oil

3 tablespoons sugar or honey

3 cloves garlic, crushed and minced

1-inch piece of fresh ginger, minced or grated

2 green onions, greens removed and white parts sliced thinly

2-3 teaspoons crushed red pepper flakes, or dried spicy peppers

1 tablespoon cornstarch

2 tablespoons peanut oil (or other preferred oil)

Additional ingredients

½ cup flour

½ cup corn starch

½ teaspoon baking soda

Peanut (or other oil) for deep frying

Salt to taste

Rice for serving

Directions

1. Begin by preparing the marinade: Combine all marinade ingredients, except for cornstarch, in a medium-sized bowl. Whisk well. Slowly add in cornstarch, whisking to eliminate any clumping. Add chicken to bowl, toss gently, cover and refrigerate for 30-60 minutes.
2. In another bowl, combine all ingredients for the sauce, except ginger, garlic, green onions, and peanut oil. Whisk thoroughly to eliminate any clumping of the cornstarch. Set aside.
3. To make the dusting for the chicken, combine flour, ½ cup cornstarch, and baking soda in a bowl. Season to taste with salt.
4. Heat 2 tablespoons of peanut oil in a hot wok. Add garlic, ginger, and scallions. Sauté 2-3 minutes. Pour set aside sauce mixture into pan. Heat to boiling, and then remove from heat. Pour sauce into a separate bowl and set aside.
5. Add enough oil to the wok to be able to deep fry the chicken cubes. Heat oil over medium-high heat.

6. Once oil is hot, remove chicken from marinade and coat in dusting powder. Make sure that each chicken cube has a thick, even coat of the flour mixture.
7. Carefully add the chicken to the hot oil, one piece at a time.
8. Cook chicken for approximately five minutes until chicken is no longer pink and juice runs clear. Coating should be a nice golden brown.
9. Remove chicken from hot oil and allow to drain. After the cooking oil has cooled remove it from the pan.
10. Add chicken and sauce mixture to the skillet. Toss gently to coat and cook over low heat until heated through.
11. Serve immediately with rice.

Pork with Snow Peas

Serves: 4-6

Preparation Time: 10 minutes

Marinating Time: 30-40 minutes

Cook Time: 15 minutes

Ingredients

1 pound pork tenderloin, cubed

1 pound snow peas, cleaned and trimmed

½ cup water chestnuts

2 cloves garlic, crushed and minced (divided)

1-inch piece of fresh ginger, minced or grated (divided)

4-5 green onions, finely sliced with greens and whites separated

2 tablespoons soy sauce

1 teaspoon rice wine

1½ tablespoons hoisin sauce

1½ teaspoons sesame oil

2 teaspoons sugar

2 teaspoons cornstarch (divided)

2 tablespoons peanut (or other preferred oil)

Salt and pepper

Rice for serving

Directions

- Begin by preparing a marinade for the pork: Combine the soy sauce, rice wine, sesame oil, sugar, green onions, approximately half of the garlic and ginger in a medium or large bowl. Whisk until blended. Add in 1 teaspoon of the cornstarch and whisk thoroughly until well blended and free of any clumping. Add cubed pork to bowl and toss gently. Cover and refrigerate for 30-60 minutes.
- Preheat wok over medium-high heat. Add enough peanut oil to coat with some residual at the bottom.

- While the oil is heating, mix one teaspoon of the cornstarch with enough water to make a clump free, thin paste. Set aside for later use.
- Add snow peas, garlic, ginger, and water chestnuts to the wok. Cook, tossing gently for approximately 1-2 minutes until snow peas start to turn a brighter shade of green. Season with salt and pepper if desired, remove from pan and set aside.
- Return the wok to the heat and add more peanut oil. Add the pork, including the marinade, and sauté until golden brown, approximately 2-3 minutes.
- Once pork is browned, return snow pea mixture to pan. Add hoisin sauce and cornstarch mixture. Toss ingredients gently to coat, and cook for 3minutes or until sauce begins to thicken.
- Serve immediately with rice.

Mu Shu Pork

Serves: 4-6

Preparation Time: 30 minutes

Cook Time: 20 minutes

Ingredients

Mu shu pancakes

2 cups flour

¾ cup water, boiling

2 tablespoons sesame oil

Filling

½ pound boneless lean pork, cut into very thin strips

½ cup shiitake mushrooms, chopped in large pieces

½ head Napa cabbage, shredded

1 celery stalk, sliced thinly

½ yellow onion, sliced thinly

1½ cup bean sprouts

1-inch piece of ginger, peeled and grated

4 cloves garlic, crushed and minced

¼ cup chicken stock

2 tablespoons soy sauce

1 tablespoon rice wine

1½ teaspoons hoisin sauce

2 teaspoons sesame oil

1½ teaspoons sugar

2 eggs, beaten

1½ tablespoons peanut oil (or other preferred oil)

Directions

Mu Shu Pancakes

- Begin by making the Mu Shu pancakes: In a bowl, gradually stir water into flour, mixing with a fork until a soft dough begins to form. Turn dough out onto a floured surface and knead until dough becomes firm and elastic. Cover dough and let rest 20 minutes.
- Form dough into a log, a little over a foot long. Cut into 1-inch pieces, and form each into a small ball.

- Flatten each ball with your hand and brush with sesame oil. Use a rolling pin to further flatten each pancake, until each is about 6 inches wide.
- In a medium nonstick skillet, cook pancakes over medium heat, one at a time. Cook until they become lightly browned, about two minutes per side.
- Set aside and cover until use.

Filling

- Add 1 tablespoon oil to a hot wok. Add eggs to the pan and cook until just set, cutting into thin strips while cooking. Set aside.
- Add remaining oil to the wok, and over high heat, add the garlic, ginger and pork. Cook, tossing gently until pork browns, approximately 3-4 minutes. Add mushrooms, celery, bean sprouts, cabbage, onions and chicken stock to the pan. Cook, tossing gently for 2-3 minutes.
- Pour in soy sauce, rice wine, hoisin, sesame oil and sugar. Toss gently, and heat until mixture reaches near boiling. Remove from heat and let it set 2 minutes.
- Serve immediately with the pancakes.

Twice Cooked Pork

Serves: 4

Preparation Time: 15 minutes + 4hrs chilled

Cook Time: 40 min.

Ingredients

½ pound pork belly

1-inch piece of fresh ginger, peeled and sliced thinly

3 cloves garlic, crushed and minced

1 tablespoon sweet bean paste

1 tablespoon chili bean paste

1 tablespoon rice wine

2 teaspoons dark soy sauce

1 teaspoon sugar

5 green onions, thinly sliced, greens reserved for garnish

1 tablespoon peanut oil (or other desired oil)

Rice for serving

Directions

- In a small saucepan, place pork belly and enough water to completely cover it. Pork should fit snuggly in pan. Bring water to boil, then reduce heat and let simmer for 20-25 minutes.
- Remove pork from water, wrap tightly and chill in the refrigerator for at least 4 hours.
- Once pork is chilled, cut it into thin strips and set aside.
- In a small bowl, combine the rice wine, soy sauce, sugar, and sweet bean paste. Whisk until well mixed.

- Preheat a wok over high heat. Add oil and pork belly. Sauté, tossing gently until pork belly begins to brown and crisp around the edges.
- Add garlic, ginger, green onions, and chili bean paste to the wok. Toss and cook for 1 minute.
- Add sauce that was set aside, toss and cook for 3 minutes over low heat.
- Garnish with scallions, if desired.
- Serve immediately with rice.

BEEF TAKE-OUT FAVORITES

Beef and Broccoli

Serves: 4-6

Preparation Time: 10 minutes

Cook Time: 15 minutes

Ingredients

2 tablespoons cornstarch

4 tablespoons soy sauce

1 tablespoon dry sherry

2 teaspoons sugar, separated

5 tablespoons peanut oil

1 pound flat iron steak, thinly sliced against the grain

1 tablespoon oyster sauce

1¼ cups beef broth

4 thin slices peeled ginger

1 head broccoli, cut into florets

1 large onion, halved and sliced ½-inch thick

3 tomatoes, quartered lengthwise

4 cloves garlic, minced

Cooked white rice, brown or fried rice, for serving

Directions

- In a large bowl, add 3 tablespoons of soy sauce, 1 tablespoon of sherry, 1 tablespoon of peanut oil, and 1 teaspoon of sugar. Whisk until incorporated and then whisk in 1 tablespoon of cornstarch. Once the mixture is smooth, add the thinly sliced flat ion steak and 1 clove of minced garlic and toss until meat is completed coated. Place in refrigerator until needed.

- In another bowl, add beef stock, remaining soy sauce, oyster sauce, and whisk in the last tablespoon of cornstarch. This will be your sauce, so let it stand until needed.
- Heat a large skillet or wok on high heat and add two tablespoons of peanut oil (heat oil for 30 seconds), ginger, broccoli, and remaining sugar. Stir the vegetables for 3 to 4 minutes and then add onion, cooking another 3 minutes. Transfer to a plate.
- Add the last of the peanut oil to the pan, and after the oil is hot, add the flat iron steak. Stir fry for 3 minutes, then add tomatoes and remaining garlic continue to stir fry for 2 more minutes. Add broccoli, ginger, and onions back into the pan along with sauce and simmer for 3 to 4 minutes until warmed through.
- Serve over your choice of rice.

Beef with Oyster sauce

Serves: 4-6

Preparation Time: 10 minutes

Cook Time: 15 minutes

Ingredients

1 pound flank slice thin across grain
1½ tablespoons dark soy sauce
1 tablespoon dry sherry
2 teaspoons cornstarch
1½ tablespoons of beef stock
1 tablespoon peanut oil
¼-inch slice ginger, chopped
¼ cup sliced mushrooms
¼ green bell pepper, julienne
1 small carrot, peeled and cut diagonally into thin slices
¼ cup bamboo shoots, thinly sliced
2½ tablespoons oyster sauce
½ teaspoon granulated or soft brown sugar
¼ cup beef stock
4 tablespoons peanut oil for stir-frying
½ teaspoon salt
½ teaspoon pepper
Rice for serving

Directions

- In a bowl, mix the dark soy sauce, sherry, 1½ tablespoons of stock, and 1 tablespoon of oil, and then whisk in the cornstarch. Once marinade is smooth, add steak and toss till steak is coated.

- In another bowl, add remaining stock, oyster sauce and brown sugar, and whisk until incorporated and set aside.
- Heat a large pan or wok on medium-high heat, and add half the oil and heat oil for 30 seconds. Once oil is heated, add ginger cooking until aromatic then add steak and stir fry until brown. Remove from pan and reserve.
- Add the remaining oil to pan and heat oil, then add carrot and stir fry for 3 minutes. Add mushrooms and bamboo shoots. Stir fry for an additional minute.
- Pushing the vegetables to the side, add sauce and bring to boil the add steak back in and simmer for an additional 3 minutes.
- Season with salt and pepper.
- Serve with your rice.

Pepper Steak

Serves: 4-6

Preparation Time: 10 minutes

Marinating Time: 2-4 hours

Cook Time: 15 minutes

Ingredients

1 pound flank steak, sliced very thinly against the grain

5 garlic cloves, minced

1 tablespoon ginger, minced

4 tablespoons soy sauce

1 tablespoon coarse ground black pepper

½ cup sherry

6 to 8 de-stemmed and crushed dry chilies

1 tablespoon corn starch

1 large yellow onion, sliced

1 red bell pepper, sliced

1 green bell pepper, sliced

½ teaspoon salt

4 tablespoons peanut oil

Directions

- In a large bowl, add soy sauce, sherry, ginger, garlic, black pepper, chilies, and corn starch. Whisk until all ingredients are incorporated. Add steak, toss until coated and refrigerate for 2-4 hours.
- In a hot pan or wok, heat three tablespoons of peanut oil on high heat. Quickly blanch the steak. Stir frying the steak for no longer than 20 seconds. Remove steak and set aside.
- Add more oil if needed and heat add bell peppers and onion and salt. Stir fry for 3 to 4 minutes or just until peppers are tender.
- Add steak back in and add the remaining marinade. Reduce heat and simmer till sauce has thickened.
- Serve over your choice of rice.

Szechuan Beef

Serves: 4-6

Preparation Time: 10 minutes

Cook Time: 20 minutes

Ingredients

1 pound flat iron steak (cut into very thin strips against the grain)

2 carrots, julienne

1 celery stalk, julienne

½ small red bell pepper, julienne

1 tablespoon minced ginger

4 green onions, white part only, julienne

1 tablespoon hoisin sauce

3 teaspoons chili sauce

6 tablespoons peanut oil for stir-frying, or as needed

¼ teaspoon salt

1 tablespoon dry sherry

½ teaspoon sugar

½ teaspoon Szechuan peppercorn

Rice for serving

Directions

- In a small dry pan, toast the Szechuan peppercorns until fully aromatic, approximately 2-3 minutes.
- In a small bowl, add chili sauce and hoisin sauce. Mix and set aside.
- Heat pan or wok on high heat, and add a tablespoon of peanut oil. Let the oil warm for about 30 seconds. When the oil is hot, add carrots, celery and red bell pepper. Stir fry for 3 to 4 minutes and remove from heat. Place vegetables on a plate and reserve.
- Add 4 to 5 tablespoons of peanut oil and add steak. Stir fry for about ten minutes or until the steak is a dark brown and sizzles.
- Splash with the sherry once the steak is done.

- Remove all but 2 tablespoons of peanut oil. Add the reserved hoisin sauce mixture, ginger, salt, and green onions. Turn heat down to medium-high. Stir fry for just under a minute.
- Add carrots back into the pan and Szechuan peppercorns. Simmer for about 2 minutes.
- Serve with rice.

Sesame Beef

Serves: 4

Preparation Time: 40 minutes

Cook Time: 15 minutes

Ingredients

2 tablespoons soy sauce

2 tablespoons dry sherry

1 tablespoon sugar

2 teaspoons rice vinegar

½ teaspoon red-pepper flakes

½ teaspoon cornstarch

1 tablespoon peanut oil

2 teaspoons sesame oil

1 pound boneless sirloin steak, thinly sliced in strips against the grain

2-3 garlic cloves, minced

1 tablespoon sesame seeds

Rice for serving

Directions

- In small bowl, add soy sauce, dry sherry, sugar, red pepper flake, rice vinegar, and cornstarch, and whisk until fully incorporated. Place in a sealable bag with sirloin steak strips. Let marinate in the refrigerator for at least 30 minutes. Drain steak onto a plate and reserve remaining marinade sauce.
- In a small dry pan, toast sesame seeds over medium heat, until the seeds are aromatic, about 1 minute.
- In a large pan or wok, heat on medium-high, add both oils and heat for another 30 seconds. Once the oil is heated add garlic and steak strips. Stir fry for about 3 minutes.
- Stir in reserved marinade sauce. Stir to coat and continue cooking for 1-2 minutes on medium heat.
- Add the toasted sesame seeds once sauce is thick.
- Serve with rice.

Kung Pao Beef

Serves: 4-6

Preparation Time: 1 hour, 10 minutes

Cook Time: 15 minutes

Ingredients

1 pound flank or flat iron steak

1 tablespoon soy sauce

2 tablespoons sesame oil

1 tablespoon dry sherry

2 tablespoons peanut oil

4 dried red chilies, split

6 garlic cloves, minced

½ tablespoon grated ginger

1 teaspoon Szechwan peppercorns, crushed

2 green onions, slice white and green parts in ½ -inch pieces
1 red bell pepper, trimmed and cubed
2 tablespoons soy sauce
3 tablespoons dry sherry
2 tablespoons balsamic vinegar
1 teaspoon sugar
1 cup vegetable broth
1 tablespoon cornstarch
½ cup roasted peanuts
Rice for serving

Directions

- In a large bowl, add the soy sauce, sesame oil, dry sherry, and 2 minced garlic cloves. Mix and the add steak to marinate. Marinate for at least one hour.
- In a bowl, make the sauce by mixing together 2 tablespoons of soy sauce, 3 tablespoons of dry sherry, 2 tablespoons balsamic vinegar, 1 teaspoon sugar, and 1 cup vegetable broth, add cornstarch, and whisk right before adding it to the steak.
- In a large pan or wok, heat on high and then add peanut oil heating oil for 30 seconds.
- Add red chilies, ginger, and Szechuan peppercorns stir fry for 1 minute.

- Add remaining garlic, scallions, and bell pepper. Stir fry for 3 minutes, and add the steak. Sauté for an additional 2-3 minutes.
- Add the sauce and simmer until sauce thickens, about 3 to 4 minutes.
- Add peanuts and stir.
- Serve with rice.

Shrimp in Lobster Sauce

Serves: 4-6

Preparation Time: 40 minutes

Cook Time: 10 minutes

Image from Goodpix.com

Ingredients

1 pound medium-sized shrimp, shelled and deveined

½ pound ground pork

1 egg white

1 egg, beaten

1-inch piece of ginger, peeled and grated

2 green onions, sliced, greens reserved for garnish

2 tablespoons black bean paste

3 tablespoons cornstarch, divided

3 cloves garlic, crushed and minced

1 tablespoon sesame oil, divided

½ cup vegetable or seafood broth

1½ tablespoons sherry

3 tablespoons soy sauce

2 teaspoons sugar

1 tablespoon peanut (or other desired) oil

Rice for serving

Directions

- In a medium bowl, combine the egg white, ½ of the sesame oil, ½ of the cornstarch, and green onions. Add prepared shrimp to the bowl, tossing to coat. Cover and refrigerate for 30 minutes.
- In another small bowl, combine black bean paste with the ginger, garlic, sugar, sesame oil, sherry, soy sauce, and broth. Whisk in cornstarch until mixture is free of any clumps.
- Heat a wok over high heat and add oil. Add the bean paste mixture to the pan, stirring until fragrant, less than 1 minute. Add ground pork and brown for approximately 2 minutes.
- Add sauce from bowl to wok, lower heat to medium-high while stirring to incorporate and to avoid lumps from the cornstarch. Once sauce is heated through, add shrimp and cook for 3 minutes or until the shrimp turn pink and are cooked through.

- To finish, pour beaten egg into wok, while stirring to influence a shredded texture to the egg as it cooks. Remove from heat.
- Serve immediately with rice
- Garnish with green onions, if desired.

Spicy Scallops in Garlic Sauce

Serves: 4-6

Preparation Time: 10 minutes

Cook Time: 15 minutes

Ingredients

1 pound scallops, rinsed and dried

2 green onions, sliced

½ cup fresh basil leaves

½ small red bell pepper, diced

1-2 small red hot peppers, sliced

5 garlic cloves, crushed and minced

½ cup chicken broth

1 tablespoon fish sauce

2 teaspoons sherry

1 teaspoon sugar

1 tablespoon cornstarch dissolved in enough water to make a thin, lump free paste

Peanut (or other preferred) oil

Rice to serve

Directions

- In a small bowl, combine chicken broth with fish sauce, sherry, and sugar. Whisk well until sugar is completely dissolved. Set aside.
- Heat a wok over high heat and add enough oil to coat the pan. Add green onions and garlic to the pan, tossing until fragrant, about 1 minute.
- Add the prepared scallops, basil leaves, red hot peppers, and red pepper, tossing gently while cooking. Cook for 2-3 minutes.
- Reduce heat to medium. Add the reserved sauce, stirring to coat the scallops. Let sauce simmer for up to 4-5 minutes. Take care with keeping an eye on the scallops, as they can easily overcook.
- Push the scallops and vegetables to the sides of the wok, leaving the sauce and cooking juices at the bottom of the pan. Add cornstarch mixture to the sauce, stirring to incorporate.
- Stir and cook until sauce thickens, about 1-2 minutes. Serve immediately over rice.

Cantonese Style Lobster

Serves: 4-6

Preparation Time: 20 minutes

Cook Time: 20 minutes

Ingredients

2 lobster tails (about 1 pound each)

¼ pound ground pork

1 egg, beaten

1 teaspoon salt

2 tablespoons all-purpose flour

2 tablespoons black bean paste

4 cloves garlic, minced

1-inch piece of ginger, peeled and grated

2 green onions, cut into 1-inch pieces

1 cup vegetable or fish stock

3 tablespoons sherry

2 tablespoon soy sauce

1 tablespoon cornstarch, dissolved in enough water to make a thin, clump free paste

Salt and pepper to taste

1 green onion for garnish, if desired

1 cup peanut (or other preferred) oil

Rice for serving

Directions

- To prepare the lobster, cut each tail in half. Leaving shells on, wash under running cold water. Pat dry with paper towels. Leaving the lobster meat in the shell, cut lobster meat into chunks no larger than 1-1½ inches. Season lobster meat with salt and pepper to taste.
- In a small bowl, mash minced garlic and add black bean paste. Mix together and set aside.
- Heat wok over high heat. Add oil to the pan, ensuring that there is enough to totally submerge lobster pieces. Once oil is heated, carefully lower lobster pieces into the oil. Fry lobster until the shells turn a red color. It is best to use the shell color as an indicator of doneness in this recipe. Take care not to overcook the lobster. Remove fried lobster from the pan and place lobster tails onto a plate lined with paper towels to catch excess oil.
- Allow any oil remaining in the pan to cool and then discard the leftover oil, except for enough to just coat the pan.
- Add black bean and garlic mixture to the wok, cook while tossing gently for no more than 1 minute. Push bean paste mixture up the side of the wok to slow further cooking.

- Add ginger, green onions, and pork. Cook, tossing gently until pork begins to brown.
- Add stock, along with soy sauce and sherry to the pan. Once liquid is warm, reincorporate the bean paste mixture back into the mix. Heat to near boiling
- Add fried lobster pieces to the pan. Toss, and cook for one minute. Cover and allow lobster to be steamed for 3 minutes.
- Remove lid and add cornstarch mixture. Season additionally if desired. Slowly pour in beaten egg, and swirl around until cooked.
- Remove from heat, and serve immediately with rice.

Mu Shu Shrimp

Serves: 4-6

Preparation Time: 30 minutes

Cook Time: 15 minutes

Image from pixgood.com

Ingredients

Mu Shu pancakes

2 cups flour

¾ cup water, boiling

2 tablespoons sesame oil

Shrimp filling

1 pound small shrimp, peeled and deveined

2 cups shiitake mushrooms, sliced

1 medium carrot, shredded

1 small head Napa cabbage, shredded

5 cloves garlic, crushed and minced

3 green onions, sliced, with greens and whites separated

2 tablespoons soy sauce

2 teaspoons cornstarch

1 teaspoon chili-garlic sauce

3 teaspoons hoisin sauce

1 tablespoon peanut (or other preferred) oil

Directions

Mu Shu Pancakes

- To make the Mu Shu pancakes, gradually stir water into flour in a bowl. Mix with a fork until a soft dough begins to form. Turn dough out onto a floured surface and knead until dough becomes firm and elastic. Cover dough and let rest 20 minutes.
- Form dough into a log, a little over a foot long. Cut into 1-inch pieces, and form each into a small ball.
- Flatten each ball with your hand and brush with sesame oil. Use a rolling pin to further flatten each pancake, until each is about 6 inches wide.
- In a medium nonstick skillet, cook pancakes over medium heat, one at a time. Cook until they

become lightly golden brown on the edges, about 1-2 minutes per side.
- Set aside and cover with foil.

Shrimp filling
- In a small bowl, combine cornstarch with enough water to make a thin, clump free paste. Add chili garlic sauce and soy sauce to the bowl. Whisk until mixture is well blended. Set aside.
- Heat a wok over high heat. Add oil to the pan to coat. Add shrimp and garlic to the pan, and toss gently. Cook for 2-3 minutes until shrimp are pink and cooked through. Remove from pan and place on a cutting board. Chop each shrimp into 4-6 pieces each and reserve.
- Add more oil to the wok if needed. Once oil is heated, add mushrooms, onions and carrots. Cook while tossing gently for 3-4 minutes. Add cabbage to vegetable mixture and cook until just wilted, about 2-3 minutes.
- Put the shrimp pieces back into the wok.
- Add prepared cornstarch mixture to the wok, toss gently to coat and stir-fry for about 1 minute to warm the shrimp and sauce.
- Serve immediately with Mu Shu Pancakes.

MAMA LI'S SPECIALITIES

Orange Beef

Serves: 4-6

Preparation Time: 15 minutes

Cook Time: 10 minutes

Ingredients

½ pound flat iron steak, sliced thinly

1 egg white

1 large orange, zested and juiced

3 tablespoons soy sauce

3 tablespoons sherry

3 tablespoons rice wine vinegar

2 teaspoons chili garlic sauce

2 teaspoons sesame oil

5 green onions, sliced, greens reserved for garnish

1 tablespoon sugar

1 teaspoon baking soda

¾ cup cornstarch, divided

Peanut oil for frying (or other preferred oil)

Rice for serving

Directions

- Brush steak with baking soda to form an even coat. Place in a bowl and refrigerate until ready to use.
- In a small bowl, combine orange juice along with sherry, soy sauce, and rice wine vinegar. Add sugar to dissolve and then add 2 teaspoon of the cornstarch, whisking until the sauce is clump-free.

- Place egg white in a shallow dish. Take meat out of the refrigerator, and toss with egg white to coat evenly. Add cornstarch gradually to the meat, tossing to coat. Keep adding cornstarch until meat has a thick, even coat on it.
- Add oil to a wok and heat over high heat. The oil level in the pan should be high enough that the pieces of meat can be completely submerged.
- Once oil is hot, slowly lower meat into the pan with a slotted spoon. Fry until coating is crisp and golden brown, approximately 3-5 minutes. Remove meat from pan, and place the beef pieces on a plate lined with paper towels to catch excess oil. Don't overcrowd the wok when cooking the beef. Depending on the size of the wok, meat may need to be cooked in several smaller batches.
- Remove wok from heat and let oil cool for a few minutes. Discard oil, keeping enough to coat the pan. Add green onions and chili paste. Toss until fragrant, about 1-2 minutes. Add prepared sauce mixture into the wok along with orange zest and sesame oil. Bring mixture to a boil and cook until thickened, approximately 2 minutes.

- Return beef to pan and toss to coat. Warm over low to medium heat until heated thoroughly, about 1-2 minutes.
- Serve immediately with rice
- Garnish with green onions, if desired.

Chicken Curry

Serves: 4-6

Preparation Time: 10 minutes

Cook Time: 25 minutes

Ingredients

1 pound boneless, skinless chicken, cubed

3 medium potatoes, cubed

1 cup fresh or frozen peas

2 large yellow onions, cut into slices

5 cloves garlic, crushed and minced

1½ tablespoon curry powder

1 tablespoon sugar

2 tablespoons soy sauce

½ cup water

1 tablespoon cornstarch, blended with enough water to make a thin, clump free paste.

½ teaspoon salt

2 tablespoons peanut (or other preferred) oil

Rice for serving

Directions

- In a small bowl, combine soy sauces, water, and sugar. Whisk until sugar is dissolved. Set aside.
- Warm a wok over high heat. Add 1 tablespoon oil to pan to coat surface. Add garlic and onions, tossing gently until onions just begin to soften, about 1-2 minutes. Remove onions from pan and set aside.
- Add remaining oil to the wok and add chicken and curry powder, toss gently while cooking for 4 minutes.
- Add soy sauce mixture to the wok. Add in potatoes, peas, and onion. Bring to boil for 1 minute. Reduce heat to medium, cover, and simmer for 15 minutes.
- Remove lid, and add cornstarch. Increase heat to medium-high. Stir while bringing to a boil until sauce thickens.
- Serve immediately with rice.

Lake Tung Ting Shrimp

Serves: 4

Preparation Time: 20 minutes

Marinating Time: 30 to 60 minutes

Cook Time: 25 minutes

Ingredients

1 pound large shrimp, peeled and deveined (shells reserved)

2 cups broccoli florets

1 cup snow peas, washed and trimmed

1 cup green beans, washed and trimmed

1 medium carrot, sliced diagonally

1 celery stalk, sliced diagonally

4 cloves garlic, crushed and minced

1-inch piece of ginger, peeled and grated

1 bunch green onions, greens reserved for garnish

¼ cup fish stock

½ cup sherry or dry white wine

2 tablespoons soy sauce

1 teaspoon cornstarch

¼ cup water plus cooking water

1 tablespoon peanut (or other preferred) oil

Rice for serving

Directions

- In a medium bowl, combine soy sauce, sherry, ¼ cup water, and cornstarch. Whisk until blended and free of clumps. Add shrimp to bowl, toss to coat. Cover and marinate for 30-60 minutes in the refrigerator.

- Add shrimp shells to a small saucepan. Add just enough water to cover the shells. Simmer over low heat while shrimp is marinating in the refrigerator. Liquid in pan will reduce, producing a flavorful broth. Drain, discard shells, and set aside.
- Heat wok over medium-high heat. Add enough oil to coat the pan. Add broccoli, carrots, celery, green beans, and snow peas. Cook, tossing gently until vegetables are crisp and bright in color, approximately 4-5 minutes. Toss garlic, green onions, and ginger into vegetables, and stir-fry one minute longer.
- Remove shrimp from the refrigerator and add to wok. Toss to incorporate and cook 1 minute. Add remaining marinade, and shell stock. Mix thoroughly, and bring to boil. Stir until sauce thickens. The shrimp should be cooked through and have changed color.
- Remove from heat and serve immediately over rice. Garnish with green onions, if desired.

Chinese Spare Ribs

Serves: 4-6

Preparation Time: 10 minutes

Marinating time: 8 hours + (overnight)

Cook Time: 1hr 5 minute

Ingredients

1 slab pork spareribs, about 4 or 5 pounds, sliced into individual ribs

5 cloves garlic, crushed and minced

½ cup soy sauce

½ cup sherry

¼ cup hoisin sauce

3 tablespoons chili garlic paste

4 tablespoons packed brown sugar

2 tablespoons molasses

1¼ teaspoons Chinese five-spice powder

½ teaspoon cardamom

1½ teaspoons sesame oil

Directions

- Place ribs in a large stock pot and cover completely with water, plus an extra inch. Bring water to boil, reduce heat, and let simmer for at least one hour. Meat should be tender and close to falling off the bone. Remove ribs from water and allow to cool completely.
- In a large bowl, combine all other ingredients. Split the marinade in two. Reserving half in a sealed container in the refrigerator. Place cooled ribs into the other half of the marinade and toss to coat. Cover and refrigerate for 8 hours or overnight.
- Let ribs rest at room temperature at least 30 minutes before cooking.
- Preheat broiler or grill.
- If using a broiler, transfer ribs to a foil-lined baking sheet. Brush liberally with remaining marinade and broil or grill for 5-7 minutes or until hot and just beginning to crisp around the edges. Turn over the ribs after 3 minutes. Brush with marinade and continue cooking for 2-4 more minutes.
- Transfer to a serving plate and enjoy immediately

DESSERTS

Almond Cookies

Makes: 24-30

Preparation Time: 10 minutes

Chilling Time: 2 hours

Cook Time: 15 minutes

Ingredients

2 cups all-purpose flour

½ teaspoon baking powder

½ teaspoon baking soda

⅛ teaspoon salt

¾ cup sugar

½ cup butter

¾ cup white sugar

1 large egg

3 teaspoons almond extract

½ teaspoon vanilla extract

24-30 blanched almonds for garnish (optional)

Directions

- In a large bowl, mix together the dry ingredients of flour, baking powder, baking soda, and salt.
- In another bowl, cream the butter, shortening, and sugar with an electric mixer until creamy. Add in egg and extract, mixing until blended
- Add the flour mixture to the creamed butter in 4 even increments, thoroughly mixing after each one. Dough will be coarse and crumbly after mixing.
- Using your hands, form the dough into two foot long logs. Wrap tightly with plastic wrap and refrigerate for at least two hours.
- Preheat oven to 325°F/163°C.

- After chilling, remove and unwrap rolls. With a sharp knife, cut each log into 12-15 even-sized pieces. Form into a ball with your hands and place on a parchment-lined cookie sheet, leaving about an inch between cookies. Push a blanched almond into the center of each cookie, if desired.
- Bake for 15-17 minutes, or until cookies are lightly golden brown on the edges, and fragrant.
- Allow to cool before serving.

Chinese Fortune Cookies

Makes: 20

Preparation Time: 15 minutes

Cook Time: 15 minutes

Ingredients

½ cup flour

1½ teaspoons cornstarch

¼ teaspoon salt

2 egg whites

½ cup sugar

½ teaspoon vanilla extract

½ teaspoon almond extract

3 tablespoons vegetable oil

3 teaspoons water

Directions

- If you haven't done so already, begin by either printing out or writing fortunes on small strips of paper.
- Preheat oven to 325°F/163°C.
- In a medium bowl, combine flour, salt, cornstarch, and sugar. Once mixed thoroughly, add 3 tablespoons of water to the mixture.
- In another large bowl, lightly whisk the egg white, extracts, and oil until mixture is frothy.
- Slowly add flour mixture into the egg mixture, stirring until smooth. Dough will be very soft, similar to the consistency of peanut butter.
- Place spoonfuls of dough onto a parchment-lined baking sheet, leaving a couple of inches in between to accommodate for spreading during baking.
- Place in oven and bake 10-15 minutes, or until cookies turn a golden brown.
- One at a time, remove each cookie with a spatula and place in a plate or if you can tolerate the heat, your hand works best. Place the fortune in the middle of the cookie and fold over, forming a traditional fortune cookie shape. Press edges down to form a light seal.
- Allow to cool completely before eating.

Chinese Doughnuts

Makes: 12

Preparation Time: 15 minutes

Cook Time: 10 minutes

Ingredients

2 cups all-purpose flour

2½ teaspoons baking powder

½ teaspoon salt

¾ cup milk

⅓ cup butter, cubed

⅓ cup butter

¾ cup milk

Oil for frying

Granulated sugar for dusting

Directions

- In a medium-sized bowl combine flour, baking powder, and salt.
- Using your hands, add butter to the flour mixture and incorporate until crumbly but with no large clumps.
- Add milk and mix until a firm dough forms.
- Turn dough out onto a lightly floured working surface and knead just enough to form an elastic ball. Do not over knead the dough in this stage.
- In a wok or pan large enough for frying, heat 2 inches of oil over medium-high heat.
- Shape dough pieces into golf ball-sized balls. Flatten slightly, not applying too much pressure.

- Fry in small batches, not overcrowding the pan. Slowly lower doughnut into oil and fry until golden brown, about 4 minutes, turning once.
- Remove doughnuts from oil and dust in sugar.
- Allow to cool slightly before eating.

CONCLUSION

My hope is that in within the pages of this book, you have found that recreating your favorite Chinese takeout dishes is not only healthy and delicious, but also remarkably easy. Many traditions and memories are created around food. The difference between ordering takeout and creating it yourself could be the creation of memories that will last a lifetime. Chinese cuisine is loved across cultures, including in America. You now have the ability to build upon this buy cooking in your own home and sharing with those closest to you.

Keep in mind that while you are cooking, that many chefs create as they go. These recipes are a guide for you, but you are the chef. Have fun with them and explore with new flavors, maybe even change them slightly to make them your own. What is it that you love about your favorite Chinese takeout restaurant? Is there something about their orange sauce, or is one of their seafood sauces that puts them over the top? These recipes will help you create dishes that rival those passed down through generations. Enjoy every moment of this new culinary journey you are on, and toss those takeout menus into the trash along the way.

ABOUT THE AUTHOR

Sarah Spencer, who lives in Canada with her husband and two children, describes herself as an avid foodie who prefers watching the Food Network over a hockey game or NCIS! She is a passionate cook who dedicates all her time between creating new recipes, writing cookbooks, and her family, though not necessarily in that order!

Sarah has had two major influences in her life regarding cooking, her Grandmother and Mama Li.

She was introduced to cooking at an early age by her Grandmother who thought cooking for your loved ones was the single most important thing in life. Not only that, but she was the World's Best Cook in the eyes of all those lucky enough to taste her well-kept secret recipes. Over the years, she conveyed her knowledge and appreciation of food to Sarah.

Sarah moved to Philadelphia when her father was transferred there when Sarah was a young teenager. She became close friends with a girl named Jade, whose parents owned a Chinese take-out restaurant. This is when Sarah met her second biggest influence,

Mama Li. Mama Li was Jade's mother and a professional cook in her own restaurant. Sarah would spend many hours in the restaurant as a helper to Mama Li. Her first job was in the restaurant. Mama Li showed Sarah all about cooking Asian food, knife handling, and mixing just the right amount of spices. Sarah became an excellent Asian cook, especially in Chinese and Thai food.

Along the way, Sarah developed her own style in the kitchen. She loves to try new flavors and mix up ingredients in new and innovative ways. She is also very sensitive to her son's allergy to gluten and has been cooking gluten-free and paleo recipes for quite some time.

More Books from Sarah Spencer

Shown below are some of her other books. To check any of them out, just click on the book cover you like. Follow Sarah and join in her great love of cooking!

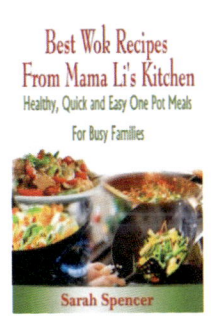

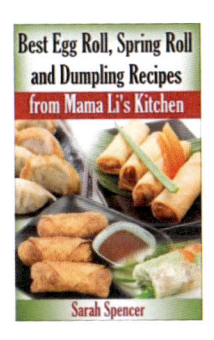

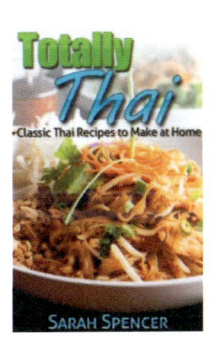

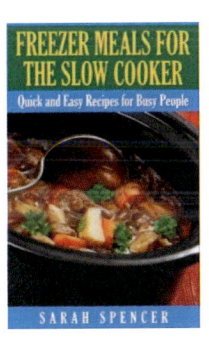

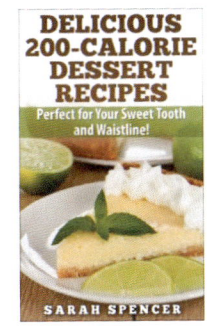

SIMPLE PALEO SALAD COOKBOOK
50 QUICK & EASY GLUTEN-FREE SALAD RECIPES
FEEL ENERGIZED, LOSE WEIGHT AND LOOK HEALTHY
SARAH SPENCER

Gluten Free TODAY
36 QUICK & EASY LUNCH AND SNACK RECIPES
SARAH SPENCER

SPICE IT UP!
THE BEST SPICE MIXING RECIPES FROM AROUND THE WORLD
SARAH SPENCER

Low Carb Dump Meals
Healthy One-Pot Meal Recipes
Sarah Spencer

APPENDIX

Cooking Conversion Charts

1. Volumes

US Fluid Oz.	US	US Dry Oz.	Metric Liquid ml
¼ oz.	2 tsp.	1 oz.	10 ml.
½ oz.	1 tbsp.	2 oz.	15 ml.
1 oz.	2 tbsp.	3 oz.	30 ml.
2 oz.	¼ cup	3½ oz.	60 ml.
4 oz.	½ cup	4 oz.	125 ml.
6 oz.	¾ cup	6 oz.	175 ml.
8 oz.	1 cup	8 oz.	250 ml.

Tsp.= teaspoon - tbsp.= tablespoon – oz.= ounce – ml.= millimeter

2. Oven Temperatures

Celsius (°C)	Fahrenheit (°F)*
90	220
110	225
120	250
140	275
150	300
160	325
180	350
190	375
200	400
215	425
230	450
250	475
260	500

*Rounded numbers

Printed in Poland
by Amazon Fulfillment
Poland Sp. z o.o., Wrocław